John Paul Jones

HERO OF THE SEAS

John Paul Jones

HERO OF THE SEAS

by Keith Brandt
illustrated by Susan Swan

Troll Associates

Library of Congress Cataloging in Publication Data

Brandt, Keith.
    John Paul Jones, hero of the seas.

    Summary: Traces the early life of the Scottish-
born sea captain who, after killing a mutineer,
sailed to America, where he became a hero of the
Revolution and founded the United States Navy.
    1. Jones, John Paul, 1747-1792—Juvenile
literature.   2. Admirals—United States—Biography—
Juvenile literature.   3. United States. Navy—
Biography—Juvenile literature.   [1. Jones, John
Paul, 1747-1792.   2. Admirals.   3. United States.
Navy—Biography.   4. United States—History—
Revolution, 1775-1783—Biography]   I. Swan,
Susan Elizabeth, ill.   II. Title.
E207.J7B86   1983   973.3'5'0924   [B]   [92]   82-16045
ISBN 0-89375-849-3
ISBN 0-89375-850-7 (pbk.)

John Paul Jones

HERO OF THE SEAS

Young John Paul sat in his favorite place—a wide stone seat under one of the windows of his home. Through the glass, he could see the sunlight glinting on the waters of Solway Firth, a gulf of water between England and Scotland. And when the air was very clear, John—who lived on the Scottish side—could see all the way across to the English shore.

For John, who was born on July 6, 1747, the view from the cottage window was always wonderful. The waters of the firth changed from one hour to the next. The gulf was gray and choppy on rainy, windy mornings, then deep blue and smooth as velvet on calm afternoons. When storms raged along the Scottish coast, huge waves reared like wild stallions tearing at the sky.

John loved the water and the many ships that sailed by. He saw the large, two-masted, square-rigged brigs and brigantines. He saw the single-masted sloops and the two-masted, swift little schooners. Their sails billowed in the breeze as the ships traveled up and down the Solway.

Schooner

Some were on their way to Dumfries in southern Scotland. Some were traveling to England. And others were on their way to cross the Atlantic Ocean to the American colonies.

John's mother, Jean MacDuff Paul, often said to her husband, "I think Johnny will someday go to sea. He watches those ships as a shepherd watches his flock."

9

John Paul, Sr. shook his head. "The lad's just four years old," he said. "It's just something for him to do. I think I'll take him out with me tomorrow. He can help me clear some brush."

Mr. Paul was the head gardener of Arbigland, an estate owned by the Craik family. The job of head gardener was an important one. Mr. Paul was in charge of a crew of workers who tended the apple orchards, the flower beds near the main house, the herb garden behind the kitchen, and the broad field of vegetables. John's father took great pride in his work. Arbigland was a fine estate, and Mr. Paul was known as the

finest gardener in the county of Galloway. This was quite an honor in an area famous for its beautiful gardens.

The Pauls were not a rich family, but there was always plenty of food on their table. Fresh fruit and vegetables came from the garden. There was salmon from nearby streams, and fresh mutton from the estate's flock of sheep. Porridge, oatcakes, biscuits, and lots of milk and cream were served every day. And for holidays, like New Year's Day, the family sat down to roast beef with bread pudding and a steaming haggis, a special Scottish dish.

Little John led a happy life. His father was a warm-hearted man with a merry sense of humor. Mrs. Paul, besides being a very good cook and housekeeper, was easy-going and loving. The five Paul children—William, Elizabeth, Janet, Johnny, and Mary Ann—were healthy and well cared for.

John liked to play all kinds of games with his brother and sisters. But his favorite games had to do with the sea. He made toy boats out of sticks and old rags. When he was alone, he would sail them on the pond near his house and make up different stories each time. One day, his boats might be a merchant fleet sailing the Atlantic to the colonies. Another day, they were pirate ships raiding a faraway port, or handsome warships with rows of booming cannons.

When John was with his friends, they staged make-believe battles. The boys dueled, using sticks as swords and daggers. They spoke "pirate" language, charged aboard imaginary ships, then fought off attackers.

Sometimes John walked to the little port town of Carsethorn, a mile and a half from his house. He liked to look at the boats anchored there. They were mostly small fishing boats, but once in a while, a large merchant vessel dropped anchor.

15

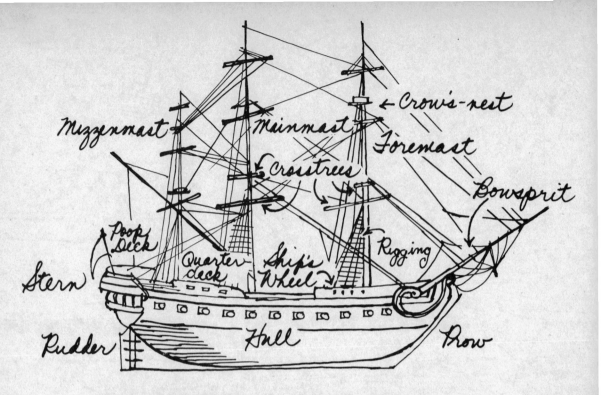

Young John enjoyed talking to the sailors and hearing about their adventures at sea. One special day, a friendly captain let the boy come aboard his brig. John excitedly gripped the ship's wheel in his small hands. He even climbed the rigging part of the way to the top. He would have gone the rest of the way to the crow's-nest, but the captain ordered him down.

"Your father would never forgive me if I let you hurt yourself," the captain said.

John didn't say anything, but he thought, *Someday I'll sail aboard a ship like this. And I'll climb the rigging faster and better than any man who ever sailed the seven seas!*

The boy wanted to learn everything about boats and seamanship. He begged an old sailor in Carsethorn to teach him to tie knots; the man agreed. He took a length of rope, showed John how to make a simple knot, then sent the boy home to practice. Not until John could tie it quickly and perfectly, without looking, did they go on to the next kind of knot.

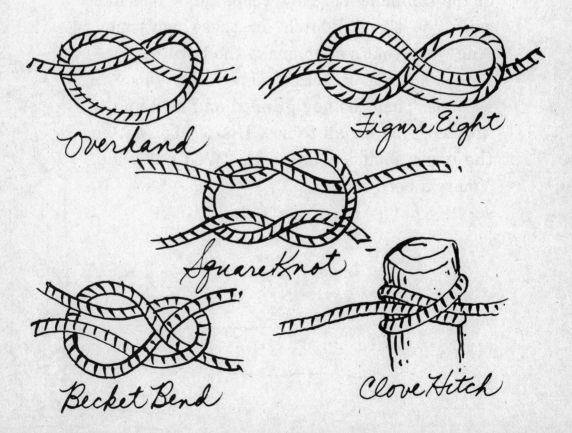

By the time he was eight, John had mastered many knots. The old sailor was pleased with his young pupil. He liked to boast about the boy's skill to his friends at the waterfront. There was a whole group of sailors whose years at sea were over. On sunny days, they sat in front of the sailmaker's shop and spun tales of the old days.

Each time John showed his teacher how well he tied the newest knot, there was a reward. The sailor took John to the old-timers' bench in front of the sailmaker's. "Now then, lad," the sailor said, "do the half-hitch for these gentlemen. And when that's done, make the bowline."

John's swift fingers finished the knots in seconds. Then the boy grinned and held up the knotted rope for all to see. His teacher patted the boy's shoulder and said, "Well done, lad! You're a born sailor."

Now John claimed his reward—a story about the sea. He heard about fierce storms, about pirate ships, and about bringing home huge catches of fish. Listening to these stories taught John many things. He learned about far-off islands where it was always hot and where sugar cane grew like grass. He learned about the icebergs in the North Atlantic and about the huge turtles near the tip of South America. He learned there were people who spoke languages different than his own.

The old sailors taught John the foreign words they had picked up on their voyages. After a while, he knew how to ask for bread, milk, and meat in six different languages. Several times, John taught his playmates some of the words he had learned. The young Scottish boys livened their talk with bits of Chinese, French, Spanish, and Swahili.

Mr. and Mrs. Paul were amused by their son's new store of words. His knots were another matter. Young John practiced on things all over the house, making life difficult for the family. One day, he tied all of the kitchen chairs to the table. Another day, he tied knots in every piece of string, ribbon, and cord in the house. Mrs. Paul couldn't put on her apron to prepare dinner until he untied the strings. Janet and Elizabeth became very angry when they found all their hair ribbons knotted.

The knot-tying finally stopped the day Mr. Paul found his supply of garden cord twisted into every kind of knot John knew how to make. Mr. Paul led his son to the pile of knotted cords. "You'll undo every one," John's father said sternly. "And you'll promise never to tie knots where they're *not* wanted, or you won't be allowed to visit your sailor friends in Carsethorn again."

John untied the knots as quickly as he could. He made the promise his father asked for, and he kept it. It was too much fun going to Carsethorn to give it up for a prank.

Except for that incident, John was really a very good boy. He was also a very good student at the Kirkbean parish school, where he went from the age of seven to thirteen years old. The school, taught by James Hogg, the minister of the Kirkbean church, was one large room. On the front wall, there was a colored map of the British Isles. A thick Bible always lay on the carved oak stand near Mr. Hogg's high, wide desk. The children sat on the backless benches and worked at long wooden tables. The youngest boys and girls were in front, and the oldest were in back.

When John went to school, there were no readers or arithmetic books. In fact, there were no children's books at all in those days. John and his classmates learned to read from the Bible and other grown-up books. One of John's favorites was John Bunyan's *Pilgrim's Progress,* a book filled with stories about how goodness is rewarded and evil is punished.

The books that John read in school had a deep effect on him. They gave him a very strong sense of right and wrong. They also shaped the way he used the English language. His writing was clear, intelligent, and powerful. Years later, John would become involved in the American Revolution, and it was, in part, due to his persuasive writing ability that an American navy was formed.

Of course, when young John sat in Mr. Hogg's classroom, copying out lines from Bunyan or the Bible, he had no idea how important this learning would be. All he knew was that he loved the flow and rhythm of a well-written sentence. He also enjoyed Mr. Hogg's style of teaching arithmetic. The class learned by counting and measuring everything in and around the town. Arithmetic came alive for the children as they counted and measured the people, animals, ships, and land of the area.

In 1756, when John was nine, his eighteen-year-old brother, William, went to America. He settled in Fredericksburg, Virginia, where he became a tailor. William wrote home often about life in the colonies. He described the beautiful, rich, untouched land stretching farther than the eye could see. He wrote about the Indians living in the forest. Most of all, he told about the wonderful feeling of freedom and democracy and opportunity for all. "Here, your talent is more important than your name," William wrote. "Lord High-and-Mighty, if he has no skills, will have the respect of none in this land. While Mr. Down-to-Earth, if he be hard-working and clever, will do well in Virginia."

William also told about the growing anger that the colonists felt for England. This was a feeling understood well by the Paul family and most Scots. Like the colonists, the Scots also wished that their country was independent from their English rulers, as it had been long ago.

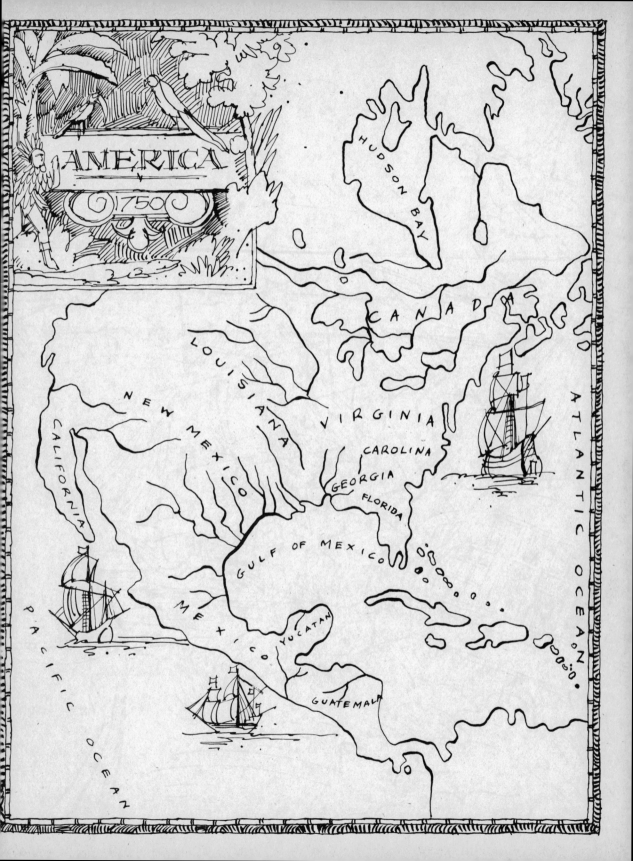

Over the centuries, the English and the Scots had fought many battles. The last crushing blow to Scotland's dream of freedom—the Battle of Culloden, on April 6, 1746—was still fresh in their minds. After that defeat, many young Scots sailed for the colonies. Among the colonial patriots crying out for American freedom were these same sons and daughters of Scotland.

Time and again, William Paul begged his parents to come to America. But they did not want to go. "It's a fine dream, but not for your mother and me," Mr. Paul told the children. "We have a snug cottage, and Mr. Craik is a fair master. And these are *my* gardens. I have tended them for many years and plan to do so until I die."

"Oh, Father, don't you ever want to travel?" John asked. "Wouldn't you like to see faraway places?"

"No, son. I'm content here," Mr. Paul answered. "But *you* can make a choice. If you wish, you can go to Virginia and join your brother. He will teach you the tailor's trade. Or you can stay right here and work with me. Then, someday, you can be head gardener of Arbigland."

"I can never be as fine a gardener as you," John said. "My heart isn't in it. Nor am I interested in being a tailor. What I want, more than anything in the world, is to go to sea."

Mr. Paul sighed. "If it is to be the sea, so be it," he said. "But there's still time for you to decide. You're only eleven. In two years, when you are old enough to be an apprentice, we'll talk about it again."

32

The next two years didn't change young John's mind. He went to school. He played with his friends. Yet no matter what he was doing, he thought about the sea. As his thirteenth birthday came near, he told his parents, "My choice is still to be a sailor. Will you help me?" They said yes.

John would have liked to join the Royal Navy. But in those days, it took money and friendship with important people to arrange a commission in the Navy. The Paul family did not have the money or know the right people. That left John one other possibility—to join the crew of a merchant ship. That is what he did, early in 1761.

John's mother packed his new wooden sea chest with warm clothing, sweet biscuits, and dried fruit. Bidding goodbye to his family, the thirteen-year-old boy boarded a small fishing boat that was crossing Solway Firth to Whitehaven. There, he signed papers that apprenticed him to John Younger, a ship owner.

For seven years, John Paul was to work on Mr. Younger's ships. He would not receive much pay, but he would get something far more important—an education in seamanship. At the end of seven years of service, John would be qualified to serve as a ship's officer.

John's first ship was the *Friendship*, a brig that carried a crew of twenty-eight. As cabin boy, John was the lowest member of the crew. He had to clean out the living quarters, wash pots for the cook, empty buckets of garbage over the side, and do any job any other crew member told him to do. It wasn't easy work, but he did it well and without complaint.

Even when a sailor screamed at him for a mistake, John kept his mouth closed. He remembered what Mr. Hogg had told him: "If you want to be a leader and have control of others, you must first have control of yourself." Sometimes the teenager wanted to talk back, but he never did. By the time the *Friendship* reached the West Indies, John had won the respect of the entire crew.

After unloading its cargo of butter and wool in Barbados, the *Friendship* took on rum and sugar. Then it set sail for Virginia, where the rum and sugar were sold. The ship was loaded with tobacco, pig iron, and barrel staves, and then set sail for home.

Young John Paul made this round trip four times. On each voyage, he was given more responsibility. It was a perfect life—Christmas at home in Scotland, the summer visiting his brother William in Fredericksburg, Virginia, and the rest of the year at sea.

In 1764, the owner of the *Friendship* was forced to sell all of his ships. He also had to dismiss all of his sailors. As a result, John was freed of his contract as an apprentice and given a fine letter of recommendation. He wasn't out of work long. He soon found a place as third mate aboard the *King George,* a trading ship out of Whitehaven. After serving on the *King George* for two years, he became chief mate of the *Two Friends,* another trader.

When John was twenty-one, he became captain of the *John,* a sixty-ton brig with a crew of seven men. In just eight years, the hardworking Scotsman had gone from cabin boy to command of his own ship! Over the next five years, his fame as a merchant captain grew. Then something happened that changed both his life and American history.

John's ship was at anchor in the West Indies when one of the crew tried to start a mutiny. The sailor rushed at Captain Paul, swinging a heavy club. John fought back with his sword and killed the mutineer. In revenge, the dead man's friends threatened to murder the captain and burn his ship. John wanted to stand his ground, but he was advised to leave—and quickly!

He bought passage on a ship bound for Virginia. Because his name was so well known, he signed the register as John Jones. He kept the name of John Paul Jones when he reached Virginia, where he stayed with his brother. It was as Jones that he met Ben Franklin, Thomas Jefferson, and other Americans talking about revolution. Soon John was also caught up in America's struggle for independence.

The situation with the British had brought the American colonies to the brink of war. When revolution seemed at hand, John used his powerful writing skills to argue for an American navy. In a letter to Thomas Jefferson and Robert Morris, he wrote, "I cannot conceive of submission to complete slavery. Therefore, only war is in sight. The Congress must meet again. And when it meets, it must face the necessity of taking those measures which it did not take in its first session; namely, provision for armament by land and sea."

Through his efforts, an American navy was formed, and John began his career in that navy as its first First Lieutenant. He quickly rose to the rank of captain, winning fame for his daring raids on seaports along the British coast.

But John Paul Jones soared to his greatest glory in September 1779, when he captained the old warship *Bonhomme Richard* against the *Serapis,* a swift forty-four cannon British frigate. John's ship didn't seem to have a chance, but his brilliant seamanship kept the battle raging for hours. After the *Serapis*'s cannons had battered the American vessel, the English captain called out, "Captain Jones, do you surrender?"

Standing beside a red-hot cannon, John Paul Jones shouted back, "I have not yet begun to fight!"

The courage of their captain swept through the tired American crew. Soon the tide of battle turned, and it was the English captain who finally lowered his flag in surrender. The American victory marked the turning point in the naval war against Great Britain. And it established the American navy as a force to be respected.

When the Revolutionary War ended, John Paul Jones was hailed as one of the heroes in the struggle for liberty. He was also famous as the world's greatest authority on organizing and running a navy. Soon, nation after nation was asking him to build them a modern fleet.

For the rest of his life, John kept saying that he wanted to retire to Virginia and be a gentleman farmer. But there was always another job to be done somewhere in the world, always another naval problem to solve. John never did find the time for that farm in America. On July 18, 1792, at the age of forty-five, he died in Paris, France.

For many years, his body remained buried in a small French cemetery. Then, in 1905, John Paul Jones was returned to his adopted homeland. With full honors, his body was buried in the chapel of the United States Naval Academy at Annapolis, Maryland. America's greatest naval hero was home for good.